PASSIVE INCOME:
The 1 in a million enormous wealth acquisition tactics in 2022

Thomas N. Nelson

All rights reserved. No part of this publication may be reproduced, distributed, or transmitted in any form or by any means, including photocopying, recording, or other electronic or mechanical methods, without the prior written permission of the publisher, except in the case of brief quotations embodied in critical reviews and certain other noncommercial uses permitted by copyright law.

Copyright © Thomas N. Nelson, 2022.

Table of contents

- **INTRODUCTION AND DEFINITION OF PASSIVE INCOME**
- **Making passive income with crypto currency**
- **6 ways you can use debt to build passive income streams:**
- **Passive Income through collectibles**
- **Passive income with online opportunities**
- **Real Estate passive income**
- **Passive Income Investor Mistakes To Avoid**
- **15 Different Ways To Create Passive Income In Real Estates**
- **Passive Income Ideas To Stop Trading Time for Money in 2022**
- **Conclusion:**

INTRODUCTION AND DEFINITION OF PASSIVE INCOME

Passive income is sometimes defined as "making money while you sleep," but there's more to it than that.

If it was so simple, everyone would be counting dollar notes while simultaneously counting sheep. If you have enough money, you may acquire assets like an Airbnb rental home, cryptocurrencies, and equities that earn money on autopilot. But what happens if you don't have the finances to get started?

The solution for many designers and bloggers is to build the assets themselves. Larger assets, like property, entail investment cash that not everyone has, but producing assets yourself requires your time and work as an investment, so you may enjoy the results later.

If you're ready to be paid absolutely nothing as you build up your passive income plan, it may be an incredible long-term revenue source and a steady cash flow. Here's a guide to passive income for beginners.

Passive Income needs no work to sustain. It might be supplementary income from a rental property, the stock market, or a business that you are not actively engaged in.

A closer look into a passive income

With passive income, you're not selling your time for money as you would do at a 9-to-5 job. Instead, you're developing or purchasing an asset that you can sell or make money with, regardless of whether you're at your desk or on a beach in the Maldives.

There are many passive income possibilities, including producing a book, developing a course, investing in real estate, and operating an affiliate marketing scheme.

But none of these activities are as passive as people prefer to imagine. You have to put in the effort upfront, like really authoring the book you're going to sell, producing the videos for your course, and picking the assets you'll acquire. And you have to do all of this without being directly paid, in the expectation that it will pay off for months or years thereafter.

Despite this, passive income may be a good supplemental money source (something that's never been more vital in a weak and improving economy).

What is Passive Income?
Passive income comprises money and losses made through a business in which a person

is not actively engaged. Examples include property renting (given real estate isn't your field of employment), equipment leasing, and limited partnership involvement.

Also,\sPassive income is any money made in a method that does not involve too much work. Various passive income-producing ideas demand a lot of effort, to begin with, like starting a blog or leasing property, but ultimately, they make money even while the owner is sleeping.

Reasons for Building Passive Income

Personal income is the biggest wealth-producing instrument — something that demands an individual's active engagement. Thus, even if an individual has a full-time job, he or she would appreciate more money without necessarily having to sweat for it.

Developing a strategy to produce passive income gives various advantages. With the increased income, a person can grow the wealth-building basis so that it is possible to take early retirement.

Additionally, passive income is a backup plan in case the individual quits their day work and gives an alternative in case a retiree outlives a retirement plan.

Making passive income with crypto currencies

This occurs to many bitcoin speculators. Cryptocurrency trading and investing may be incredibly rewarding, but also quite time-consuming. The profitability is in no little part owing to the volatility of the market. This might generate worry for investors. It's all owing to the ongoing need for consumers to check their portfolios and attempt to profit from possibilities. Managing this type of economic structure is no simple feat.

Many investors are unaware that cryptocurrency may produce passive income. The only plan of many investors is to acquire bitcoin, Ethereum, or other cryptocurrencies. Next, they wait for the value of these assets to grow. Historically, this argument has shown, at times, to be right. However, it also implies that money is locked. During the same era, these investors may have substantially enhanced their financial capacities. They elected not to do so.

Passive revenue is produced directly from ownership over your digital assets. It requires no continual effort. Instead, it asks that customers make a few wise decisions at the outset of their trip. The strategy is analogous to compounding interest, reinvesting income, or renting investment assets. Passive crypto income is conceivable in 2022 since the industry comprises a plethora of enterprises trying to compete with the existing financial sector.

Why your crypto assets should be working for you:'

It is never a good idea to have money in idle condition. People are frequently pushed to change their cash into a valued asset via inflation. Or, at the very least, they should consider it. While some individuals invest, others believe it's too hazardous.

Stocks are typically a dangerous venture and demand a lot of prior knowledge about the topic. Many individuals acquire immovable assets such as real estate to create passive income through renting. This is a terrific concept. However, it implies additional issues with managing these resources.

Crypto culture does not always encourage adopters to make revenue from existing assets. The properties of liquidity and decentralization, however, may contribute immensely to accomplishing precisely that. Decentralized Finance (DeFi) technologies sought to revolutionize the crypto environment. It made passive income more profitable and simple than ever before. These prospects influenced many investors. Let's take a deeper look at the strategies that each crypto-enthusiast might use to create a passive income from their digital assets.

How to create passive income using cryptocurrencies

There are several options to explore when wanting to create a passive income from cryptocurrencies. Each brings distinct potential, as well as problems that need to be recognized. Some are more lucrative than others. At the end of the day, however, if done properly, any approach might offer you a hefty crypto profit gained without work.

Lending and yield farming are among the most popular methods to make passive income using bitcoin. Both entail contributing part of your digital assets, for a brief period, towards a crypto project. In exchange, you will earn a fee equivalent to the amount you have loaned.

Other passive income techniques

Mining is another prominent way. Currently, the basic PoW style of mining is no longer economical for most users. Instead, cloud mining may be a terrific solution. Crypto staking is another strategy to take advantage of your digital assets.

Let's also not forget about crypto savings accounts. These crypto firms will pay a yield to individuals willing to put monies into the accounts.

The passive income opportunities do not end here. There are also affiliate programs and airdrops that are worth examining. Running a lightning node may be an alternative for people interested also in the technical elements connected with blockchain technology. Users may also acquire dividend-earning tokens that will offer them a stake in a corporation. All of these are alternatives worth examining. All of these take a significant bit of inquiry.

To spare you some of the research efforts, we have collected a list of the most lucrative techniques. Let's look at them and how each one may give you crypto revenue.

Ways to get passive income with cryptocurrency

1. Staking\sProof-of-stake is a blockchain consensus technique. It lets dispersed network members agree to fresh data being added to the blockchain.

In many respects, staking is the purest method of receiving a passive income from crypto. It is an alternative or perhaps a substitute for the function of the crypto miner. And it may be incredibly lucrative for users over time.

How the earnings happen
Blockchains provide open, decentralized networks that enable people to participate in the governing process. This is engaged in

validating transactions. This is essential because it reduces the need to have central authority such as banks. Blockchains may randomly pick participants and raise them to the level of validators. In exchange, they are rewarded for their efforts.

Instead of "miners," who earn new block rewards as in Proof-of-Work (PoW), the validators obtain new block rewards in Proof-of-Stake (PoS) (PoS). While validators don't require pricey hardware, they must have enough tokens to be qualified for the next block on the chain.

How much you will gain from staking relies mainly on the coin itself. The value of the tokens being staked might grow over time. Historically, this has occurred on various occasions. This also includes a certain level of danger. If the token's value drops, so do your profits. Making the proper decisions, initially, will considerably enhance your chances of becoming successful.

Cosmos (ATOM), Tezos(XTZ), and Cardano (ADA) are some of the most popular cryptocurrencies that may be staked at the current moment. All of them are also accessible on prominent crypto exchanges.

How staking is designed
Essentially, the validators earn incentives on staked cash in exchange for their contribution to the network's authenticity. This validation process is known as Proof-of-Stake. It permits holders (those who are in it for the long term) to generate passive income.

Several systems choose validators. They may be utilized in many ways. Some blockchain networks demand that users deposit or commit financial resources. A blockchain picks validators from a pool of users who have staked a specified quantity of its native digital asset.

Crypto staking is an excellent strategy to earn crypto rewards. It is also a fantastic opportunity to support the ideology underlying blockchain technology. Focusing on staking is a wonderful technique for the long-term adoption of bitcoin. Even in 2022, this may be highly rewarding.

2. Yield farming
With the emergence of decentralized exchanges and smart contracts, yield farming became increasingly popular in 2020–2021. The system depends on users contributing to the financial liquidity of the protocol.

Investors deposit tokens into a unique smart contract called a liquidity pool to obtain the reward. The liquidity pool's traders earn a share of the fees they create. This is a mechanism to contribute to a decentralized trading system and gain incentives for it.

How the earnings happen

Yield farming is another method to make passive crypto revenue. These are achievable because of the dynamic operations and liquidity of decentralized exchanges. Trading platforms exist that enable customers to depend on smart contracts. These are programmed self-executing computer contracts.

In turn, investors may receive the liquidity that they require. Users do not trade with brokers or other traders. Instead, they trade against money that investors have put into the liquidity pools. Liquidity providers, in turn, earn a percentage of the trading fees from this pool.

The interest rate relies on a variety of things. On a good day, farming returns might have an Annual Percentage Yield (APY) of 30% on well-known coins. The incentives might be considerably larger for lesser-known currencies aiming to create a reputation.

However, the method is not without its pitfalls. First of all, consumers need to consider price volatility. This is especially significant for the lesser-known coins that we discussed. Furthermore, rug pulls also need to be addressed while approving these tactics.

How to yield farming is designed
You will need to become a liquidity provider (LP), to start generating passive revenue via the yield farming system. The mechanism frequently needs Ethereum and a DeFi token such as Uniswap or PancakeSwap. You may also need to hold a stablecoin such as Tether (USDT) to get started.

After you deposit liquidity, the decentralized exchange will send LP tokens that represent your part of the total liquidity pool money. These LP tokens may be staked on compatible decentralized lending systems to earn extra interest. This technique offers you two interest rates for a single deposit.

Overall, in 2022, yield farming is one of the most popular ways for making passive income from crypto.

3. Cloud mining

Cloud mining lets you mine bitcoin utilizing the cloud computing capacity that is leased. Essentially, you are using somebody else's computer to mine cryptocurrencies, such as bitcoin. It is a system worth considering in your bid to earn passive crypto income. However, it requires a good deal of forethought and calculations.

You don't have to install or run any software. Cloud mining firms enable consumers to register an account to engage remotely in bitcoin mining. This makes it more accessible to everyone throughout the world. This form of mining may be done remotely, and it eliminates the need for equipment maintenance and direct energy expenses.

How the earnings happen
Cloud miners might become members of a mining pool where they buy "hash power." In return, customers pay for the service. Participants are entitled to a proportional part of the revenues depending on the quantity of hashing power hired.

What is the interest rate? This, once again, depends on a variety of things. Primarily, you will need to look at your everyday expenditures and the projected profits. The most optimistic investors believe that with an investment of $2000, they can make roughly $100 every day while mining with a 14.33 Th/s capacity for Bitcoin.

The technique may be more lucrative, though, depending on the currency being mined and the expenses involved.

How cloud mining is developed
Cloud mining is comparable to pool mining. There you may either acquire extra

resources for your CPU or share yours. With cloud mining, you buy hash power. The miners get what is left over. You just pay for the hash rate that you pick at the start. Based on the hashes that you purchased, you receive a portion of what miners produce.

The most prevalent sort of cloud mining is hosted mining. This concept enables users to lease or acquire mining gear at a miner's location. The equipment is maintained by the miner. They are the ones who ensure that it operates as planned. Customers have direct control of their cryptocurrency via this arrangement. Because of its scaling approach, mining farms can lower the high costs of power and storage. However, this sort of mining comes with a large upfront expense.

4. Crypto savings account

Savings accounts are another conservative, typically secure approach to gaining passive income from cryptocurrencies. Users may receive a return on crypto deposits by creating a crypto savings account. They function similarly to the financial products given by normal banks.

These forms of interest-bearing digital asset accounts are still a novel crypto idea. Their rate of return is excellent. It typically puts bank yields to shame. Your APY will fluctuate depending on whether you pick a flexible or fixed term. In a word, this option enables you to make use of crypto assets that you want to store for a long period. They are more lucrative than bank deposits and are worth investigating.

How the earnings happen
High return or interest rates are the major reason to adopt a crypto savings plan. Various firms give yields of 10–20% during this period. Modern banks can't compete

with these stats. Banks frequently give a cheaper interest rate.

These savings accounts pay annual returns. These accounts, unlike banks, estimate their returns using bitcoin. Crypto assets might vary. It is crucial to keep this in mind. This may affect the yearly yield. Offers that are based on stablecoins could be better.

Simply said, organizations that provide various sorts of savings accounts are already addressing the requirements of different types of clients. You might pick accounts that give additional protection against asset volatility. At the same time, you might welcome price volatility and try to earn a higher profit.

How crypto savings account is built

The way savings accounts function is fairly easy. What you will need to evaluate is the various possibilities when it comes to taking out your cash. Flexible or fixed periods will be available for withdrawals from savings accounts. Fixed terms will enable you to lock your money up for a particular amount of time and obtain greater interest rates. These savings accounts are analogous to crypto staking's huge returns.

Users earn interest on crypto in exchange for a deposit. The best interest rates are generally found in stablecoins such as Dai (DAI) and U.S. Dollar Coin (USDC) (USDC). These sorts of discounts are given by a variety of crypto firms such as Celsius and BlockFi.

Once again, this method is particularly advantageous for anyone intending to stay involved in crypto for a long period. It is a typically safe approach to make passive income on your previously held assets.

5. Crypto loans

Crypto lending is another fantastic means of ensuring that your digital assets do not lie around idle. You will be making a profit by providing liquidity to other crypto users. The loan will be paid back to you, with interest, with a Defi platform serving as the middleman.

You may borrow or lend digital money using Defi services such as Aave or Compound. Alternatively, you may employ central finance (Ceci) networks such as Celsius. Essentially, you will be utilizing a Defi platform to become the liquidity source in a crypto loan.

6 ways you can use debt to build passive income streams:

Most individuals regard debt in a bad way. But the smart use of debt to acquire income-producing assets is a proven way toward growing wealth. I utilized this simple idea to drastically improve my net worth in a reasonably short amount of time.

These methods include,

Buy Rental Properties with Financing

Use Debt to Buy Alternative Cash-Flowing Assets

Use Debt to Finance Passive Income Businesses

Buy Dividend Stocks or Bonds on Margin\sCashback Credit Cards

Peer-to-Peer Lending

That's a lot to cover, so let's get into it!

1. Buy Rental Properties with Financing

This method is the single largest source of my wealth, therefore I will invest a little time in it. I have been investing in real estate for some years now and presently own nine investment homes. I acquired all of them with mortgages from banks and people.

In my instance, I had to pay roughly 20% down, but nowadays lending restrictions have softened and you just need to put 15% down.

Why is this method such an effective wealth-building tool? Because it combines the strength of debt with the cash flow, appreciation, and tax benefits given by real estate.

Here's an example showcasing the great power of employing leverage to acquire rental properties:

Joan has $100,000 and invests in 6 rentals. Each is worth $100,000 and she makes a 15% down payment ($15,000) on each of them. So she utilizes $90,000 for down payments and has $10,000 left over to handle repairs and other needs.

Her aggregate mortgage amount is $510,000 and her homes are worth $600,000. At the end of 10 years, her properties are valued $862,857 (assuming an increase of 3.7%, which is the growth rate of property prices over the preceding 20 years). Her total mortgages are $394,877 (assuming a 3.5% interest rate, which is market at the time of this writing).

If you deduct her mortgage from the value of her home, she has $467,980 in equity.

And this does not take into account all of the "cash flow" (which is simply revenue minus costs) that Joan has been getting on her rental properties for 10 years. On average, I see between $100 and $200 per property in cash flow each month.

Going back to our example, if Joan produced $150 in cash flow each month for each of her properties, she would have made $108,000 over ten years. And to top it all off, part of that income flow may be insulated from taxes owing to her ability to deduct depreciation as well as other costs linked to her rental properties.

So if we put together her $467,980 in equity with her $108,000 in cash, you have a total worth of $575,980 from her original investment of $100,000 (*$90,000).

That's an annualized return of about 20.4%. Imagine she had put that $108,000 in cash flow into the stock market or real estate again to further boost her returns.

I believe you get the picture.

This is the method that placed me on a new financial path.

Rental Properties Can Be Passive

Profitability is undoubtedly vital, but rental property investment also may be designed to be passive.

I self-manage my properties and they are quite hassle-free at this stage. I have a team of contractors who I contact anytime one of my properties needs repairs or upkeep and they take care of it. When a lease ends, I have someone ready to touch up the property. I have a mainly automated method for filling vacancies as they emerge.

Of course, the rentals are not fully passive even with these protections in place, but I don't spend much time or energy maintaining my properties at this point.

I invest on average roughly 5 hours each month on my rentals. Most months, it is less than 1 hour (I adore it when things are calm!). When vacancies emerge, it might take more than 10 hours per month since I prefer to handle my showings for potential renters.

Cars

You can purchase a vehicle (with 100% financing in many circumstances if you qualify) and rent it out on car-sharing services like Turo or Hyrecar.

Extra Storage Space

You may rent out your additional storage space (basements, garages, bedrooms, even closets) through platforms like Neighbor.

What a wonderfully passive approach to generating additional cash! Even if you don't have a spare room currently, you may purchase a shed or other storage building on your property (and finance it) to rent it out for profit.

ATM Machines

You can finance (100% is feasible) and acquire ATMs, which you may position at different places to create passive income. Every time someone uses the ATM, you will collect a charge. Occasionally, you will need to reload the machines with cash (which you may outsource) (which you can outsource).

Can be a fairly great passive revenue set-up. Check out these two articles to learn more.

ATMs for Passive Income

Vending Machines

You may also acquire (and finance) vending machines and put them up in high-traffic places. As with ATMs, you will need to replenish them from time to time, but that may be outsourced. I know folks that earn over $100,000 per year with this method.

Inflatable Bounce Houses

The beautiful thing about bounce houses is that they are reasonably inexpensive to purchase (which makes financing them simple – even a credit card will suffice) and they are quick to put up and dismantle (making it easy to outsource the work-intensive element of the company) (making it easy to outsource the work-intensive part of the business).

Plus, it is simple to do this on the side (simply arrange appointments on the weekends or when it fits you) (just schedule appointments on the weekends or when it suits you).

Billboards

This is another asset that you may acquire with financing, which can provide passive income for you. Finding a good site is crucial here — there are several regulatory limits on where you may post billboards.

Blogs

No list of passive income techniques would be complete without blogging. The approach is straightforward. Buy an established money-making blog and collect checks.

Starting a blog is a lot of hard work and it takes time to produce money, but purchasing one that has all of the posts published and is providing regular revenue might be a fantastic method to obtain a significant passive income stream.

Of course, there are financing possibilities as well. For example, internet website marketplaces like Flippa provide financing choices, including SBA loans.

Given how blogs are priced (typically with prices ranging between 25-40 times monthly net sales), you should have no issue meeting your loan installments with the money from the site (and then some) (and then some). But, as usual, perform your due research and validate the statistics before purchasing!

If you don't have the finances to purchase a blog right now and don't mind putting in the effort to create one, check out my post on How to Start a Blog From Scratch.

I cover all of the major topics you need to know, including how to set up your website and most importantly, my best methods for creating amazing articles, gaining visitors to your blog, and monetizing that traffic.

Use Financing to Buy Passive Income Businesses

Another approach to leverage debt to produce passive income is by founding (or purchasing) enterprises that can be operated passively. Some firms simply have inherent benefits when it comes to being operated passively.

One notable example is laundromats. Machines handle the heavy job of washing and drying garments. The same applies to in-bay automated vehicle washes (in fact, you see them unsupervised all the time at 24-hour gas stations) (in fact, you see them unattended all the time at 24-hour gas stations).

Just as with the alternative income-producing assets, these firms may be funded too.

Laundromats for Passive Income\sAutomatic Car Washes for Passive Income

FedEx Routes for Passive Income\sBread Routes for Passive Income\sBuy Dividend Stocks or Bonds on Margin

Another approach that leverages debt to produce passive income is purchasing dividend-paying stocks or bonds using a margin. The usage of margin may be a new idea for some readers, therefore let's review the fundamentals of margin accounts.

What Is a Margin Account?

The basic brokerage account only enables you to acquire investments up to the amount of cash you have in the account.

But if you ask (and are granted) for an upgrade of that account to a margin account, then you obtain access to what is a line of credit from the broker that may be used to purchase more securities. You may normally borrow up to half of the entire purchase price of the assets in your account. (as long as those investments are suitable for margin) (as long as those investments are eligible for margin). Source: Schwab.com

Eligible investments generally include equities, bonds, ETFs, and mutual funds.

How Do You Use Margin to Create Passive Income?

As of this writing, several brokers are giving extremely low-interest rates on their margin accounts (Interactive Brokers is renowned for this) (Interactive Brokers is famous for this). This presents an arbitrage opportunity for you. You may borrow cash on margin to acquire dividend-paying shares or bonds.

If your payment from the stock or bond is more than your interest on the margin account, you can pay off the accumulated margin interest and keep the difference.

There may not be much left, particularly if you are purchasing cautious equities or bonds with lower returns, but it's something and this is about as passive as you can go.

Note: Margin calls are still a danger if the underlying stocks or bonds decline in value, so act with care.

Cash Back Credit Cards

This one's a bit of a variation on the utilization of debt to produce passive income, but it works. I utilize it to produce a few thousand dollars each year.

The passive income technique with cashback credit cards is simple:

Get a cashback credit card that gives a respectable cashback rate (2% appears to be very acceptable)

Put as much of your spending as you can on your rewards cardPay down your balances in full each month (can't goof this part up!)

Collect the cashback rewards for some good passive income

Peer-to-Peer Lending

This one's also a bit of a variation in the approach. In this situation, you utilize debt to produce passive income, but you're not the one getting into debt.

Instead, you lend individuals money via peer-to-peer lending networks like Lending Club, Prosper, Peerform, Upstart, etc., and receive the interest payments from the loans you make.

Conclusion

So there you have it, six methods to leverage debt to generate passive revenue streams.

Of course, you should be cautious whenever you utilize debt. But if you locate a successful, income-producing asset that is reasonably low risk, utilizing debt (responsibly) to purchase it may be a terrific method to produce some additional passive income.

Why Should I Use Debt to Create Passive Income?

Using debt to produce passive income might get you more money more quickly. Debt is a potent lever and accelerant when it comes to investing results.

Here's a basic example:

If you have $100, you can purchase a passive income investment that costs $100. If your investment produces 10% in the first year, you now have $110.

But if you have $100 and use it as a down payment or a source of collateral to purchase an investment that costs $1,000 and that investment earns the same 10% return, you now have $200.

That's a 100% return compared. a 10% return.

Now, I hate to make this point again, but I have to provide a very clear caution here. Just as debt may accelerate and magnify your profits, it can also accelerate and magnify your losses.

If you borrow to acquire any income-producing item and that asset underperforms (or doesn't perform at all), you may be in danger. More hassle than if you had acquired the item without incurring debt. So carefully examine the dangers and rewards of leveraging debt to build passive income streams before taking the jump.

Passive Income through collectibles

Collectibles are anything of value that people could, well, collect—from stamps, money, and vehicles to the increasingly fashionable rare digital art known as non-fungible tokens (NFTs) (NFTs). Investing in collectibles is a terrific way to diversify your portfolio while also owning something you enjoy.

Can collectibles produce the same returns as equities, bonds, and other standard investment classes? That varies. Typically, the value of a collection is in the eye of the beholder, and like any other investment, there's no assurance you'll earn money.

What Are Collectibles?
Collectibles may be described as objects that are worth more today than they were when they were initially sold. Art, antiques,

stamps, literature, coins, trading cards, and comic books are typical sorts of collections. Rare treasures frequently demand higher prices, and the value of collectibles tends to rise with time.

Take, for example, the ultra-rare "Rabbit," a stainless steel sculpture made in 1986 by artist Jeff Koons, which sold at auction for a record-breaking $91.1 million in May 2019. It's still the most expensive piece of art ever sold by a living artist.

Other goods are mass-produced and become collectibles—Beanie Babies, anyone? Believe it or not, some of these plush, pellet-filled yard sale treasures may still be worth something (to someone, anyhow) (to someone, anyway). A recent eBay search found a listing for the 1997 Princess Diana Purple Bear with a $900,000 "Buy It Now" price.

Ideally, collectibles should stimulate the enthusiasm of the collector. An original Babe Ruth baseball card is certainly going to be worth a lot more to someone who's into baseball and collecting vintage sports cards than someone who couldn't care less about the history of the sport.

Nostalgia also has a part in a collectible's value. Nostalgia cycles tend to emerge in 20- to 30-year waves. That is to say, anything that's trendy today, like apparel or collectible toys, has the potential to become valuable 20 or 30 years in the future when individuals acquire the desire to reconnect with their history.

There are no promises that'll happen, however. In other words, if your retirement plan entails accumulating today's top-trending things in the hopes that you'll become wealthy by selling them to nostalgic Gen Zers two or three decades from now, you may want to explore another approach.

Finally, pricing is frequently dictated by a collectible's condition. Even the tiniest fault might wipe away it's worth. Again, the same antique Babe Ruth card will attract a greater price in its original and flawless condition than one that may be rendered useless because of a few scratches or a bent corner.

Collectibles Are Alternative Investments
Collectibles are regarded to be an alternative investment, a collection of financial assets that fall under the "other" category. Put another way, alternative investments aren't conventional suspects like equities, bonds, mutual funds, or cash.

Here's the difference: When you put your money into conventional investments, like stocks, you hope that they'll produce income payments or profit (or) (or both). Collectibles, on the other hand, have no inherent worth.

"Collectibles are generally susceptible to the preferences, emotions, and perceptions of purchasers and sellers, which are often ephemeral and may shrink overnight," says Rob Drury, executive director of the Association of Christian Financial Advisors.

While investing in "alts," as they're known, may be thrilling and gratifying, it can also be hazardous. With collectibles, there's zero assurance that you'll recover your original investment or that you'll be able to sell it in the future for more than it's presently worth (it's worth mentioning this is also a risk issue for many other investment items).

Collectibles and Fraud
The world of collectibles also has a dark side riddled with frauds, con artists, and fraud. For that reason alone, you must be on watch so you don't get ripped off. Understanding how to screen merchants and identify between real and fake collectibles may not

only save you money but might spare you a lot of misery.

Take this terrible story, for example, The family of a retired New Jersey fireman found out the hard way he'd been cheated out of hundreds of thousands of dollars. After he died, his family realized that the sports memorabilia collection he'd spent more than $100,000 building—including balls and bats autographed by Mickey Mantle, Babe Ruth, and other baseball legends—was full of fakes.

All were sold to him by the same dealer, who'd acquired credit and celebrity by acquiring the personal collection of New York Yankee Joe DiMaggio. That merchant ultimately became known for selling bogus baseball memorabilia.

Potential Rewards of Investing in Collectibles

Of all, not every collectibles investment ends as a cautionary story. When acquired carefully, with serious study, collectibles have the potential to develop in value and give better-than-decent returns.

You don't have to spend hundreds of thousands of dollars to gain those advantages, though. For instance, take this recent research on "Star Wars" collections from Self Financial, a fintech startup focused on helping individuals create credit. It's no wonder that one of the greatest and longest-standing franchises of all time—the first movie, Star Wars: Episode IV – A New Hope, was released in May 1977—also has a tremendous collection of collector gems.

Some of the goods sold for only a few dollars 40 years ago. Today, Star Wars items might be worth thousands. For example, assume you'd acquired an original 12 Back Vinyl Cape Jawa action figure for $5 back in 1980. In immaculate condition, the iconic toy

Jawa might bring upwards of $7,739 today—and gain of 4,000%, according to Self Financial's research

Another oft-cited example is the inaugural issue of The Amazing Spiderman comic. Stan Lee's classic narrative of Peter Parker, a high school pariah turned superhero by a radioactive spider bite, sold for a measly $0.12 when it was originally published in 1962. In 2011, ComicConnect.com CEO Stephen Fishler sold a copy for an eye-popping $1.1 million.

Advantages of Investing in Collectibles

Diversification. Collectibles may give your portfolio diversity. It's usually advantageous to put your eggs in more than one basket, instead of investing exclusively in equities and bonds.

Portability. Collectibles are tangible assets. You may hold rare collectible coins in your palm, for example. You can also transport them simply, so you may sell or trade treasures anywhere in the globe.

Follow your passion. Unlike a share of stock or bond investment, you get to enjoy your collectibles while waiting for them to increase in value. You may hang a rare picture on your wall, or drive a vintage automobile on weekends.

Fun. True collectors indulge in the excitement of the hunt—searching for the thing of their desire is near as fulfilling as acquiring it.

Easy access. Getting your hands on memorabilia is quite straightforward via online markets such as eBay or local shops. If you know what to look for, you may even be able to pick up goods of worth at yard sales, thrift stores, or pawn shops.

Downsides of Investing in Collectibles

Rampant fraud. As indicated above, unless you're an expert, collectibles are exceedingly dangerous. It's an uncontrolled business full of scams, fakes, and forgeries, and even experts may be duped by a convincing knock-off.

Markups. Collectibles merchants are infamous for marking up objects so they may make a profit. Unlike collectors, most dealers don't have the luxury of purchasing and retaining an object that may or may not improve in value. They need to make a sale so they can pay their expenses and refill inventory.

Tough comps. When purchasing and selling collectibles, it's a good idea to check the current prices for comparable goods. Bear in mind, however, that if a similar item is assessed at $5,000, it doesn't indicate yours will be valued in the same range. A collectible's value relies heavily on its condition and rarity.

Lack of liquidity. Collectibles are mainly illiquid since cashing out hinges on your ability to locate a buyer willing to pay your asking price.

Damage decreases the value. Any scratch, flaw, or imperfection may lead a once-coveted item to fall in value or become worthless.

You have to store and insure valuables. If you don't keep them correctly, collectibles may quickly be harmed by sun or water damage and other threats. And the expense to insure them is roughly 1% to 2% of the item's worth, every year. So a $10,000 item would cost roughly $100 to $200 a year to insure.

No revenue stream. Investments like stocks and real estate may offer an income in the form of dividends or monthly rent payments while you wait for their prices to improve. Not so with a collectible—you have to keep it until you can sell it.

How Are Collectibles Taxed?

A short note on taxes: The government isn't a lover of purchasing and selling collectibles, thus their sale is severely taxed.

If you've possessed a collection for more than a year, it may be liable to a maximum long-term capital gains tax of 28% when you sell it. That's noticeably higher than the 15% capital gains tax for typical assets like equities and bonds. If you sell a collectible after having it for less than one year, you'll be taxed at your regular income tax rate.

The amount you owe the Internal Revenue Service (IRS) is determined by your basis—the price you paid for the collectible when you purchased it, plus any auction or broker costs. You may also add to your base any money you spend repairing, renovating, or maintaining your item. Subtract your basis from the selling price—you'll be taxed on the difference.

Should You Invest in Collectibles?

Collectibles aren't for everyone. They're dangerous and speculative and need in-depth study and a decent bit of expertise to genuinely be effective.

If you're sold on investing in collectibles, consider receiving professional guidance and dealing with reliable sellers. It's a good idea to contact your financial adviser to understand how these assets may affect your portfolio and estate planning. Know what you're purchasing, and where the market is headed. Don't spend more than you can stand to lose if the collectible doesn't deliver the profit you intended. Finally, find delight in possessing the goods you collect, and don't acquire them with the hope that they'll return anything except years of happiness.

Another thing to bear in mind is that collectibles are illiquid, taxable investments that don't provide an income until you can sell them. They may also lose their worth in a heartbeat if broken, damaged, lost, or stolen.

If you're motivated to acquire a collectible, it should be something you love and can afford, and something you won't mind keeping onto, maybe forever

Passive income with online opportunities

How can you create passive income online?

What does it mean to produce passive income online?

It implies you make money when you are not at work, but enjoy a vacation paradise in an exotic place. Sounds fun, right?

It is not only about producing passive income through the internet, it is growing more popular online and offline. But how can you earn such a type of income?

When asked, "how do you get additional money?" Most individuals respond with "find a second job or work additional hours."

Regardless of the time issue, it is, of course, far better to work smarter than of working more. It is vital to select a strategy that would help you to generate money with minimum effort and investment.

In other words, establish a passive income!

I'll reveal how you may do this and start to produce passive income online without any work. I am confident you will discover at least one way that will suit you. You will discover how to generate money in 2022, how to produce passive income online.

Are you curious? Let's dig right in!

Earn Passive Income Over the Internet With These Easy Ways

If you want to generate money in 2022, we have a few terrific passive income options for you. Below is a list of methods to generate money online, passively and effortlessly. Despite the huge diversity, you undoubtedly had heard about some of them previously. Go over them all and select the ones that are ideal for you.

Are you ready to generate passive income online?

1.Start creating YouTube videos.
Making films for YouTube is a fast-growing sport. Nowadays, you can video from anywhere with high-quality cameras, even on your phone. And the videos you produce may actually be about anything. Think about beauty, sports, bitcoin, and someone's everyday life (vlogging or maintaining an online journal) (vlogging or keeping an internet diary).

You will spend a lot of time generating videos, particularly while they are still susceptible to editing. When done, though, they may provide passive revenue online for a long period. You will profit using "Google

Adsense" adverts that are featured on your videos.

Who can educate you better to become a super YouTube, than PewDiePie with his 100M subscribers?

You get paid every time someone looks at or clicks on this ad. The price per view is minimal, we are not talking about insane money here, but if you have many views, it is becoming a greater stream of cash, particularly when you publish material regularly.

Big Youtube stars, whose videos garner hundreds of thousands of views every day, are generating a full-time income only from Youtube.

2.Create a website for affiliate marketing.
Another extremely fascinating approach, particularly for folks with an established blog or website: is affiliate marketing. You

may use this to add links on your blog that advertise items. For example, you will get a certain sum or percentage of the sale for every purchase made using your link. Do you have numerous visitors who are interested in particular items or services? Then you can undoubtedly generate a great passive income with affiliate marketing!

There are several sites where you may identify firms that handle affiliate marketing. They aim to sell something, ideally via as many channels as possible. If your website gets enough traffic, those firms are willing to do business with you. However, you may also build a highly specialized micro specialty website that will earn cash with even lesser visitors.

The ideal method to start a website or blog is to select a subject you are passionate about, then market items or services that are related to this niche. That enhances your conversion rates! Read more about performance marketing software.

3.Sell your images on the internet.

Do you enjoy photography? If so, you may be able to make a great amount of passive income with your images. You may submit photographs taken on so-called stock photo websites, such as Shutterstock or iStockphoto. This manner, you will get a certain sum or percentage for every buyer who buys your images via that website.

If you construct a beautiful portfolio, you may earn a significant quantity of money from it. Posting your images is not difficult. The total procedure is completely automated. And the amazing thing is… any shot you take may be sold again and again and produce compound money. Ideal, right?

Keep in mind that your images ought to be exceptionally nice and of great quality. It is sensible to look at what is already in great demand. So design them somewhat with a commercial tilt; this works best 9 times out of 10!

4.Write an ebook
Writing an ebook sounds like a lot of effort at first... and it is! But once done, it may be a profitable source of money. Your book may be sold on your own website, but also, e.g., via Amazon or ClickBank. This way, you reach a big audience in one go, but make sure that your e-book is worth reading.
Photo by Lisa Fotios

You may write about anything, but you must know a lot about the topic. Give the reader a lot of helpful information, utilize the proper phrases, make it engaging and simple to read. Have you ever gotten across an issue that no one is writing about yet? Then you could have a gold mine in your hands.

Even with 1 decent book, you may generate a solid passive income for a long time... since the sales might be endless!

5.Sell your own stuff.
Creating your own items might be regarded as a fairly wide subject, where you can sell just about everything. You may manufacture your own things or have them made inexpensively in nations such as China.

You will have to construct your own website for this, where people may buy the merchandise. Another approach is to put things on Amazon, which enhances the probability of even more purchases.

Always make sure that you have your own website anyhow.

When you offer your own items, you have larger profit margins, more independence, maybe more market control, and numerous sales chances. This manner, you may easily earn more sales through huge platforms (such as Amazon) (such as Amazon). They may even provide the whole processing of your orders, providing you more time for marketing and innovation.

Regardless of the time you put in, this is an excellent source of passive income!

6.Adopt a blog that already exists
Are you able to acquire an established blog for a decent price? Then you may also generate a very excellent passive income with this blog. Blogs are being produced all the time, but not all of these blogs are utilized to their maximum potential.

So make good use of this notion.

You can accomplish this using Google Adsense and affiliate marketing. Blogs with a lot of authority and monthly traffic are great for this. In financial words, you should retain around 24 times the monthly revenue of the blog's price. If the income is $300 per month (ideally stable for many years), then you have a price of $7200. It is, of course, preferable if you can manage with less.

Pay attention to whether it is genuinely a wonderful blog, or if the owner wants to get rid of it for another reason. Savvy affiliate marketers generate $10k from their websites, so there is certainly some possibility for generating money!

7.Start an e-shop

Starting an e-shop is also an excellent option, where your own items are not necessarily needed. Starting an e-shop in a niche where your passion lies – makes it more enjoyable and lucrative. You may start small... then when all goes well, extend your portfolio with additional related goods.

You have to put a lot of effort into it, but you will produce more and more passive income.

However, don't you want to be busy with your eshop, all the time? Then you may automate a variety of procedures. For example, you may choose dropshipping, where things flow straight from the producer or wholesaler to your clients. You can also place the storage of products at Amazon or ShareASale and have the complete fulfillment arranged by these parties. This saves you time, and you also get a lot of "exposure" for your products.

Plenty of features that may take some time in the beginning, will create passive income online later on autopilot!

8.Be a referring resource.
Any tiny (start-up) company may leverage recommendations, which lead to higher sales. Make a list of businesses that you routinely turn to and those you can suggest

to others. Then, ask them whether they provide you any form of commission when people come to those firms via you. It may lead to a wonderful side-stream of money.

You may also develop a website for this with suggestions or quotes (something like a gateway) (something like a portal). Also, utilize social media and other internet avenues to improve awareness. When you approach it a bit wiser, your profits might quickly mount up.

It is, of course, crucial that you do not spend too much time on it. But it fairly simply generates a snowball effect. In this method, you also build up actual passive income, and you may do other exciting activities while the money is being made on autopilot.

9.Create an app
You may also start developing an app. Yes, I realize it's not for everyone, but it's not

THAT hard. You have to ask yourself a lot of questions.

What do you want your app to accomplish?
How do you make the app interesting to users?
What issue do you solve with it?
How do users' lives get easier with your app?
And how are you going to advertise your app?
Of course, many developers desire to create an app, so it truly stands out.

It begins with a wonderful concept, but then you also have to invest time developing it. Your app might be complicated, but yet incredibly basic. Think about those games that literally don't make sense, yet have a terrific playtime. Using the inclusion of adverts, you may generate a lot of passive revenue with applications.

You may acquire under-developed software for a very modest price, which will mount up with large usage. This manner, you may generate money for years with 1 developed app.

If you are a newbie, eager to get started take a look at this full video tutorial:

10. Develop an online course
Everyone's an expert at something, so why not develop an online course for this? It may be a terrific source of passive income!

You may approach this in numerous ways. For example, there are websites like Udemy.com, with millions of students seeking for new online courses every day. You may also submit your online course on many other websites, including Amazon, of course. There are numerous sales channels where you can sell an online course, simply utilize Google to see what fits best.

Now it is vital to design an amazing online course. If you upload your online course on foreign sites, you will have to create it in English. The use of video courses, checklists, short e-books for help, graphics, and, for example, an audio version to reinforce your information.

Also, create 3 separate bundles with appropriate pricing categories. This manner, you reach every consumer, so that you take full advantage of the customers' volume and make more.

10.Google Adsense
Google Adsense truly is one of the easiest methods to make passive income online. You install adverts on your website or blog and don't have to do anything about it.

The cash is made every time when people click on your adverts.

Although you only earn a few cents every click, it might build up when you receive a lot of visitors. The proportion that clicks on it every day might therefore go from excellent pocket money to a complete monthly income.

So it works best when you have a website that is highly viewed. It may also assist to take over an existing website. You may also integrate Adsense extremely nicely with, for example, affiliate marketing or other income methods. This manner, you build up more and more money with one website.

What are the greatest areas for Google Adsense?

Pay care to where you position the advertising. The optimal placements for this on your website are

within the content\in the header\and the sidebar's left side

Also, make sure you utilize the suggested dimensions that Google uses. And utilize advertising with graphics, but also with text just. According to measurements, the combination generates the most!

Donations

Placing a contribution button may potentially lead to passive revenue. It may not be a continuous source of money, but it may build up.

You labor hard on your website, without possibly being paid. Some guests are willing to provide you with help. When this occurs consistently, you may earn good with it.

The greatest strategy is to update fresh information consistently and to be highly beneficial for your readers. In this approach, you build up a community piece by bit... so that folks are also more motivated to make a gift.

You may use Paypal for this, for example, by establishing a contribution button with your account (or simply create one first) (or just create it first). And then publish it on your website. Most individuals have a Paypal account and can send some money for free and promptly.

You may also collect contributions on Youtube.
You may also collect contributions on Youtube. In addition to a passive income on YouTube with your films, it is an alternative option to create revenue rapidly!

It commonly occurs in live feeds, where you may occasionally watch the numbers climb substantially. Ok, you will have to build a large audience first. But there is a very strong probability that they will offer you anything. Suppose you conduct a 1-hour live webcast in which you answer queries. Then you may earn a great additional penny with this. And your live broadcast may be seen again later, when you insert adverts again. So do you routinely blend conventional videos with live streams? Then you may make money in 2 ways.

With contributions, it is, of course, true that you receive them. It is fantastic when your subscribers make a contribution. This provides you more for all your efforts.

11. Selling advertising space

Do you have a website or blog with many visitors? Then you may also make advertising space accessible for firms who wish to promote on your website. For example, you may post a banner in the header for a certain price every month. With a few banners, you make a lot of money.

12. Create manuals

Are you seeking for new methods in which you may make passive income? Then authoring manuals could be your cup of tea.

You may make quite lengthy guides for the most particular subjects. A guidebook assists individuals to reach a given objective step by step. Usually, this is accompanied by a nominal cost.

Another method is to give the handbook for free, utilizing a different income strategy. Think about Google Adsense, affiliate links, subscriptions, or other things.

It's a clever method to generate additional money!

13. Invest in real estate via crowdfunding
Investing in real estate is a highly effective technique to make passive income on the internet. However, owning a home or apartment is not particularly inexpensive. You will thus need to have equity capital or borrow it from the bank.

But there are other ways to do it differently. For example, you may invest in real estate via crowdsourcing. You don't have to put in a significant amount straight once, and you may start with a few hundred euros.

For example, if you check at the Fundrise.com website, you will discover that roughly 8.7 to 12.4% interest may be generated with this. You do not have a guarantee for a certain percentage, but you will make more money nevertheless.

14.Investing in stocks

Buying stocks might potentially provide passive income online for you for a long period. In many situations, you purchase shares, and you also claim a portion of the profit (dividend) every 3 months. Are you planning to acquire shares? Then do this from firms that are dependable and likely to create more and more profit. Photo from energepic.com on Pexels.com

You may also learn more about how stock markets function. That manner, you will be better equipped to purchase stocks at a low price. Certainly, there is not always anything wrong with the firm for the bigger corporations when shares are down. If the shares then move up again, you may take advantage of the rises.

Depending on how much you invest, you might make a significant passive income for a longer length of time!

15. Borrowing peer-to-peer (P2P) (P2P)
It's probably not your first notion to make passive income online. But it may be lucrative to borrow peer-to-peer. You get interest on money that you lend to others.

Some persons are not qualified to borrow via standard financial services companies. However, certain platforms lend it to that makes humans conceivable. You may register yourself, and in that manner, lend money to others. This does not even have to be really significant numbers.

You will then get interest on the borrowed money.

In most circumstances, it will give you some additional money, but also carefully examine the hazards. There are several classifications, including low risk, medium risk, and high risk. They show the danger of guaranteeing the loan. So pay attention to this!

16.Make money with activities you already do
You can earn money with things you already do. This includes reading emails, purchasing online, and surfing the internet.

Of course, it does not bring in much, compared to the other options listed. But it is a strategy to earn something additional, for which you do not have to do anything extra.

However, we encourage taking alternative methods.

What are the greatest strategies to make passive income online?
There are various methods to produce passive income.

Our recommendation is to concentrate on the serious techniques with which you genuinely create an internet company. They do take you some time in the beginning. But you will make (a lot of) money online rapidly and for a longer length of time!

You will constantly have to do something for it, but when everything is running… you will be extremely delighted with the outcomes accomplished.

Do you too wish to make passive income online?

We've shown you many various methods you may earn money online without having to do too much time for it, allowing you a lot of time for other enjoyable or fascinating activities. Continuous passive income 2020 trends are continuously changing, but you can always discover something that fits you.

The list is as full as possible so that you may select a manner that fits you best. That way, there is something for everyone!

How to generate money in 2022?

If you want to earn money in 2022 nothing has changed much since 2021, nevertheless, it is reasonable to assume that following the coronavirus epidemic more and money people are turning to affiliate marketing and online income prospects.

How to generate money online in2022?

Making money online in 2022 is easier than ever before since most people are turning to digital advertising, earning money from top referral programs, affiliate marketing, and blogging.

Passive income websites for sale?

If you are looking for passive income websites for sale, it's best to check places like Namecheap marketplace or Flippa, where people are selling established websites, which already generate passive income.

How to earn continuous passive income 2022?

The only option to create ongoing passive income in 2022 is to develop a mini specialized company and acquire authority in your industry. You may generate money via affiliate marketing, selling advertising space, or even through programmatic adverts.

Is it possible to generate money online 2022?

Sure! The main difficulty with generating money online in 2022 is that the competition is great and it may appear like certain affiliate marketing areas were oversaturated. However, you may counter this by directing your efforts at a smaller specialty website.

What are the best ways to make money in 2022?

The best ways to make money in 2022 are still promoting affiliate marketing products through trusted affiliate networks, selling advertising space, freelancing or starting your digital business.

Is it possible to make a digital advertising service residual income?

If you are running a digital advertising service, it's possible to make residual income from the advertising alone, however you will still need to be actively engaged in your business, closing deals, getting new clients, and sending payments. The income is absolutely passive though and can make a nice side hustle.

Real Estate passive income

What is real estate passive income?

How to start investing

Types of real estate passive income

Passive income real estate is recognized as one of the finest strategies to earn an extra source of cash, achieve stability in retirement, and finally, construct a path to reaching financial independence. However, passive income real estate investment is not always the ideal option for every individual. Would you wish to take a more active part in real estate investment or a more passive position? Read on to discover everything about passive income real estate and see whether or not it seems like a suitable match for your investment personality type.

What Is Passive Income Real Estate?

Passive income real estate is a technique by which an investor may make revenue without needing to be actively engaged. The phrase "passive income" is used loosely since the degree of necessary work and commitment varies according to the investment type. Some frequent instances of this real estate revenue are rental properties or profits produced through investment portfolios.

Why Do You Need Passive Income?
Passive income is a terrific method to generate money without having to actively work for it. Collect passive income while you enjoy your life Instead of wasting your day working for someone else. Here are some ways you may put your passive income to use:

Fund your children's college money

Set up and grow your retirement savings

Pay off your debts

Achieve financial freedom

Build your savings

What Is Residual Income?

Monthly residual income is the money that remains for a person or firm after all costs are paid, meaning the money that is left over. You may earn extra residual income via assets such as real estate. By investing in real estate, you will earn monthly cash flow that will develop your residual income over time. The one-time contribution that an investment needs will be repaid to you over time when the investment produces income.

How To Invest In Passive Income Real Estate

Passive income may be a terrific method to augment your present income and help you develop money streams to assist protect your retirement years. One of the most common methods to make real estate passive income is via rental homes. Investors that play their cards well may produce consistent revenue from rental income, but they also can make modifications to the property and grow equity.

There is a frequent fallacy that passive income real estate investment involves little to no labor. However, people interested in earning passive income with real estate should take an active part in what should be considered a company. Whether it be browsing through homes, screening renters, hiring a property manager, or resolving maintenance, owning passive income properties does need a certain degree of effort. This particularly holds for individuals who seek to maximize their revenues.

One of the secrets to constructing a successful passive income real estate investment requires planning and having a good company strategy. This means versing yourself in your desired area, whether it be the same neighborhood as your current house or even out-of-state so that you know local real estate trends and prices. The knowledge you acquire from the real estate market can assist you to pick out the greatest feasible market to hold a passive income property, as well as finding property listings that promise strong cash flow.

After the research phase transfers into the implementation phase, you will also need to have a plan in place on how you will handle renters, money, paperwork, and the property itself. As you can see, passive income real estate is quite a complicated process, and maybe the word "passive" is a bit disingenuous. However, with lots of preparation, study, as well and understanding of the correct questions to ask or common errors to avoid, you will be well on your way to a smart approach that may make your life much simpler in the long run.

Passive Income Investor Mistakes To Avoid

Passive income may be a great wealth-building strategy when developed correctly. However, many investors make blunders that impair their long-term passive income potential. Follow these suggestions to make sure you avoid beginner blunders when it comes to passive income:

Not having adequate financial flow: You may have heard the saying "cash is king," and any passive income real estate agent will tell you the same. When owning a rental property, your major aim is to acquire value while producing continuous cash flow. However, the market might vary over time and affect your value. Cash flow becomes your bottom line in terms of delivering an income and being able to take care of your property.

Failing to carefully screen renters: One of the greatest methods to enhance your passive income from real estate is by leasing only to the finest potential tenants. A poor tenant might turn out to be considerably more costly than any vacancy, such as via property damage or even a protracted, expensive eviction procedure (or worse, a lawsuit) (or worse, a lawsuit.) Take the time to screen your renters carefully, and be sure to verify their records and references.

Not being ready to become a landlord: Newbie investors could adopt the method of a passive income real estate investment vehicle without recognizing that being a landlord is a challenging business that should not be taken lightly. Be careful to realize that managing rental properties should be addressed as if it were a small company.

Not collecting rent quickly: new landlords need to be extremely explicit about regulations and hold renters responsible for obeying these rules from the very beginning. Tenants may take advantage of their landlord's compassion and build a habit of being late on rent payments or even have trouble catching up. Waiting too long to collect rent can not only damage your cash flow but may also lead to a lengthy eviction procedure that can lead to heated sentiments on either end.

Not maintaining an active part in management: Even when working via a property management firm, an owner should actively manage their property by staying in frequent communication with renters and providing regular care and repair of the property. Although this may entail more time, effort, and money, it will help safeguard your bottom line in the long term. Proper management of a property may assist decrease tenant turnover, boosting property value, and eliminating needless maintenance expenses.

Keep Tenants Happy
Whether you choose to manage the property yourself or with the aid of a professional, be sure the renter's requirements are being fulfilled. Ensure each apartment is in excellent shape before new tenants move in and react to urgent repair requests. Many landlords also advocate contacting renters every few months to check in with tenants on the state of the property. This proactive strategy may help keep renters pleased and keep your rental money coming.

15 Different Ways To Create Passive Income In Real Estates

The various advantages of passive income may have you asking how to earn passive income for yourself. However, passive income may seem different to everyone, according to Nate Tsang, Founder, and CEO of WallStreetZen. "Passive investing is putting a one-time investment into an asset and just waiting for the money to grow. This may be in the form of rent if you're investing in real estate, dividends if you invest in equities that pay dividends, or just a continuous buildup of wealth with something like an index fund," according to Tsang.

There are several avenues you may pursue that will lead you to passive income sources. Take a look at the real estate investment ideas that can do so:

Single-family units: Those asking how to produce passive income in real estate might start with the most frequent of instances. Perhaps the easiest sort of property to grasp, a single house or condo may be acquired and leased to just one renter. Single-family renters tend to assume greater psychological ownership over the house, causing them to take better care of the property. However, while empty, a single unit will bring in no revenue at all.

Duplexes, triplexes, and more: Properties with two to four units provide comparable advantages to single-family apartments while giving a lesser necessity for extensive maintenance as compared to apartment complexes. Due to the higher number of tenants, these properties might be a bit more difficult to maintain than a single-family unit but give a superior cash flow perspective. The risk of a prospective vacancy is dispersed among numerous units instead of simply one.

Apartment buildings: This building type is commonly used for structures with five or more apartments. Investors may take a business loan instead of a residential loan and benefit from economies of scale. However, they should be prepared for more extensive management or to employ a property management specialist.

Commercial buildings: Commercial properties may be leased to retail tenants with long-term leases, therefore guaranteeing a more consistent source of real estate revenue. However, commercial renters might be more difficult to replace and prefer to heavily adapt the property to their business demands. Investors should expect extended vacancies, as well as having to absorb the expense of upgrading areas between renters.

Mixed-use developments: Demand for mixed-use development projects has risen consistently, and may offer a home for residential, office, retail, industrial, and institutional tenants. Investors might enjoy a range of real estate revenue streams and lease terms inside one property.

Industrial complexes: Although residential properties tend to spring to mind with the notion of passive income, assets aimed toward the business sector should not be neglected. Commercial warehouses, storage, or manufacturing facilities may offer stable performance while needing minimum supervision. It should be remembered that tenant churn might lead to protracted vacancies.

Self-storage facilities: Self-storage facilities continue to be very much in demand and can be found almost anywhere in the U.S. All facility expenses and vacancies may be distributed among numerous units, amounting to a relatively cheap per-unit cost. However, these facilities need customer service and management personnel, typically manning the premises for longer hours. In addition, proprietors should consider security and insurance expenditures.

Mobile home parks: Mobile homes provide an appealing housing choice for people under economic duress or in locations where property costs have risen. Investors that operate a mobile home park often own the land while receiving rentals from homeowners who choose to install their mobile homes on the site. Because this venture is extremely capital-intensive, investors will frequently go into the acquisition as a member of a fund or many partnerships.

Land lots: Investing in land in itself may be a distinct specialty and can be utilized to upgrade or divided up to be sold as smaller lots. This technique may be beneficial if the investor discovers a parcel of land in an up-and-coming location that will shortly be developed and sells it for a profit. However, land may be hard, since there are relatively few options to earn an income while it lies idle.

Vacation rentals: A property could masquerade as an excellent short-term or vacation rental prospect, particularly in areas with a strong transitory population, as well as tourism attractions. Investors who own a vacation rental may frequently charge more on a per-night basis than they would with a long-term renter. However, holiday rentals need continual scheduling, dealing with cancellations, paying for cleaning services, and fretting about quiet seasons.

Real Estate Investment Trusts (REITs): REITs may be looked at as a mutual fund and allow people an option to engage in the real estate market while being fully passive.

The goal of REITs is generally high-end or commercial properties and might change in association with the overall stock market.

Tax liens & deeds: The government retain the right to confiscate property when taxes are unpaid. Investors have the potential to purchase up tax lien properties at a large discount but should only take action if they have a good plan in place.

Note investments: Homebuyers have the option of taking out a house loan in the form of a private note instead of a traditional loan. There is a substantial industry involving the purchasing and selling of these notes, some of which are overdue. Investors may acquire performing and non-performing notes from other owners at a discount. This gives them the right to collect monthly payments or seize possession of the property if the property owner fails to make payments.

Hard money lending: Investors that have adequate liquidity might contemplate privately lending money to enable other persons to acquire property who guarantee to pay back the principal at a high-interest rate. The end-user is typically a fix-and-flip investor who requires rapid access to funds to pounce on a project. However, there is always a chance that the transaction may not go smoothly, and the borrower will default.

Property rehabs: Fixing and flipping houses demands more active participation in real estate investment, but may be highly successful. Properties situated in a potential rental market, but are not up to par in terms of look and condition, might go through a renovation phase before being leased out.

Passive Income Ideas To Stop Trading Time for Money in 2022

Side Hustle Nation is focused on enhancing your profitability. To achieve this, we typically work with firms that share that objective. If you join up or make a purchase via one of our partners' links, we may get compensation—at no additional cost to you. Learn more.

I set out to produce the finest dang passive income ideas piece on the Internet.

Because here's the thing…

Most "passive income ideas" blogs rehash the same boilerplate ideas—open a high-return savings account, for example.

And sure, it will generate a modest amount of passive income, but my bet is you're looking for something a little more significant.

In this piece, I'll:\sShare my personal genuine passive income sources.
Present more solid passive income ideas you can take action on today—and back them up with real-life examples.
Break down the 4 forms of passive income and why it's so vital to start creating now.
Ready?

Let's dig in.

1. Earn Affiliate Commissions
I started my start in affiliate marketing back in 2004, and it's been a substantial piece of my earnings pie ever since.

How affiliate marketing works is I receive a commission for introducing leads and consumers to other businesses and services.
Suggested Playlist: Affiliate Marketing

Make money online by sharing relevant items and services with your audience. Here's a terrific soundtrack filled with practical tips from professionals.

My first affiliate business was a comparison shopping site for footwear. It helped people find the best price on their next pair of shoes and earned commissions from Zappos and other retailers when people made a purchase.

Once the site was built, I earned these commissions whether or not I was actively sitting at the computer.

Here's a look at my daily affiliate commission trend back in the day:

Even today, affiliate marketing is a really important revenue stream for me. This site (and yes, this post too) includes lots of affiliate links to products, apps, services, and software I think will be helpful to my audience.

Here's an (over-the-top) example of an article monetized via affiliate links. Still, over its lifespan, it's generated over $40,000 in commissions. From one post!

2. Write a Book
It's never been simpler to make a book of your own and put it up for sale on Amazon.
It's one of my favorite side hustles and one of my most passive cash sources. Write the book once and get royalties for months or even years whenever it sells!

When you price your book between $2.99 and $9.99, you'll get a 70% royalty. Outside of that range, it's 35%.

For every Kindle book you produce, it makes sense to add print and audiobook versions. Thankfully, Amazon makes this exceedingly simple with their KDP Print service and ACX, the Audiobook Creation Exchange.

3. Buy Dividend-Paying Stocks
Investing in dividend cash flow has helped me get off the sidelines and into the market. (I'm the one who constantly believes we're due for a correction!)

My primary approach has been to acquire shares in firms with lengthy records of paying—and increasing—dividends. These include name-brand firms like Target, Chevron, AT&T, and Proctor and Gamble.

These "boring" old firms aren't going to experience rapid share price increases, but they do churn out constant passive cash flow.

4. Sell an Online Course

Again this goes under the idea of "create something once, and sell it over and over again."

What might you teach? Consider what others already ask you for assistance with. What do you know more about than the typical person?

With platforms like Teachable, it's never been simpler to develop and sell an online course of your own. These may attract premium pricing ($100-$2000 or more) and enable you to serve more individuals than you could with one-on-one counseling.

Over the years on The Side Hustle Show, we've seen individuals make money with online courses on just about every subject conceivable. Some of the most innovative case studies include:

Piano
Microgreens farming

Sourdough baking
Motorcycle repair
Getting ready in the morning\sand so many more!
How will buyers discover you? If you don't have an audience, one approach to attempt is the YouTube-to-evergreen-webinar strategy.

5. Rent Out Your Extra Space

You're certainly acquainted with Airbnb and similar services, where you can convert the spare space in your house into additional income. Check the calculator on their site to see how much you may make.

This becomes more passive if you have a second home and engage a 3rd party firm to handle your reservations, guest contact, and cleaning.

But if you don't want to deal with visitors at all, the Neighbor platform could be worth a look. Neighbor lets you keep people's spare items where you have room for it.

This is expected to be extremely passive monthly revenue after the first drop-down. Some hosts are making up to $10,000 a year operating their own little self-storage companies.

6. Sell a Digital Product
Several years ago, I decided to attempt selling a number of my books on Fiverr. I assumed that would be another intriguing "buy button" platform to explore with.

Sure enough, people purchased them. And in fact, they continue to buy them.

Similarly, Jodi Carlson reported making over $5k a month providing digital activity guides for Girl Scout unit leaders. She'd created a blog detailing the things she was doing with her scouts, largely merely as a reference for herself and other area leaders.

Before long, army commanders on the opposite side of the country had found her blog via Google and Pinterest. They emailed asking what other suggestions she had.

That's when Jodi started putting her activity guidelines into PDF docs. She published them to Teachers Pay Teachers, a portal to purchase and sell lesson plans, and earned many transactions in the first week.

7. Create Print on Demand Designs

This is a low-overhead, low-investment technique to create a little passive income. In our family, Merch by Amazon is a nice little side company and makes roughly $60-200 a month for us.

How it works is you upload t-shirt (and now other product) designs to Amazon, and the e-commerce behemoth handles the rest. When someone orders it, they'll print it in the size and color requested, then mail it to the buyer. You earn the margin between whatever price you set and the cost to print it.

8. Collect Ad Money from YouTube

If you have over 1000 subscribers and complete a few more conditions on your YouTube channel, you may activate advertisements and start to be paid.

Lately, this passive income flow has been approximately $500 a month:

This is the revenue source I'm probably most enthusiastic about right now since it feels entirely fresh.

And to be sure, it takes effort to develop the movies, but once they're online, they might generate passive revenue for you for years—as several of mine have.

9. Buy Commercial Real Estate\Fundrise is a fantastic "alternative" approach to investing in real estate.

With only a $10 minimum investment, you can start establishing a portfolio of pre-vetted commercial properties.

10. Earn More Interest
US Treasury Bonds presently pay 9.62%! The method to acquire these savings bonds is a touch laborious (it's the government—is anybody shocked?), but the hassle may be worthwhile to guard against inflation.

Individuals may acquire up to $10,000 worth of these per calendar year. You may cash them in after 12 months, but lose 3 months of interest if you don't retain them for at least 5 years.

If you need a bit more liquidity, try considering a DeFi (decentralized finance) platform like Gemini. When you make a deposit, the site transforms it into stablecoins – cryptocurrency tethered to the US dollar. Then they give you 6-8% interest on your account.

You may withdraw back to your bank account at any moment and there are no minimums.

Compared to the interest rates elsewhere, this has been a significant victory. For example:

Our Capital One savings are generating 1.2% interest.
"High yield" CIT Bank offers "up to 0.80%".
Our free checking accounts with Chase are paying .01%.

11. Make Short-Term Real Estate Loans
With PeerStreet and Groundfloor, you assist real estate flippers to pay their purchase and

renovation expenditures. In return, you get 6-9% passive income on your investment.

The significant benefit over other peer-to-peer lending is the loans are guaranteed by the actual property. That means if the borrower stops paying, you have some remedy - notably foreclosure.

The loans are shorter in duration, often 1 year or less, instead of 3-5 years.

PeerStreet is likewise presently only limited to accredited investors, however, Groundfloor is open to everyone and has far lower minimums.

12. Let Banks Give You Free Money
Credit card rewards are one of my favorite passive income ideas since I get them simply from spending money as I usually would.

In our home, this stream is worth hundreds of dollars a year in the form of cashback, free Amazon gift cards, and vacations.

The magic truly occurs when you take advantage of particular sign-up offers for new cards. You may earn the equivalent of 20%, 30%, or 40% cash back or more in travel value or a statement credit.

Here's simply an extremely basic example:

Credit cards like the Capital One Quicksilver Card provide a $200 sign-up bonus once you spend $500 in your first 3 months – with no annual fee. That's up to 40% cash back!

If you know you're going to spend $500 in the next 3 months, that's free money. This card also provides you with one of the best cash-back rates, with a limitless 1.5% back on every dollar you spend.

13. Get Easy Cash Back

Aside from credit card rewards, I utilize various cash-back applications to generate "reverse passive income" every time I spend. Among them are:

Capital One Shopping - A free browser plugin that helps you locate better discounts and promo coupons when you purchase online. (Even if you don't bank with Capital One.) Plus, you'll earn points you may exchange for gift cards.

Disclosure: Capital One pays me when you download the Capital One Shopping extension via my link.

Fetch Rewards – Scan your supermarket receipts using the free Fetch app to get cash back on 250+ brands. Not 100% passive but quite painless.

DOSH - Link your bank and credit cards and receive automatic cash back at selected retailers and restaurants.

14. Share Your Data

While not a large money-maker, this easy passive income strategy might be worth $200 a year or more. I felt because I'm probably already giving my data away to "big tech" for free, it would be wonderful to get paid for it.

For example, it took roughly 5 weeks to earn my first $10 worth of points on Surf—a free browser plugin that rewards you for sharing your online activities.

Other passive income options in this area include:

Nielsen Computer and Mobile Panel - Earn up to $50 a year sharing your Internet use patterns.

MobileXpression - Earn a free $5 gift card after your first week.

Savvy Connect - Earn up to $5/month per device (computer, tablet, and smartphone) (computer, tablet, and smartphone).

15. Play the Substitution Game to Save Money

I just moved to Mint Mobile, which operates on the T-Mobile network, for my mobile phone service. When you pre-pay, it costs just $15 a month:

Compared to my former supplier and my even older provider, this means savings of $180-500 a year.

Similarly, if it's been more than 2 years since you last looked for vehicle insurance, you're paying too much.

Check out Insurify for a fast and straightforward comparison of vehicle and house insurance. It'll take only a few minutes and consumers report saving an average of $489 each year!

What additional regular monthly expenditures may you minimize by bargaining with your service provider or by searching for a comparable service?

16. Refinance High-Interest Debt
According to Nerd Wallet, the typical family with debt is facing:

$6500 in credit card debt
$27,000 in automobile debt
$46,000 in student loan debt
If you're paying any non-mortgage interest right now, I would prioritize eliminating that monthly expense before exploring these other strategies. Take a peek at our partner Credible to discover more about your possibilities.

17. Buy a Rental House
Roofstock specializes in pairing investors with "turnkey" rental homes around the nation.

A few friends of mine have acquired many residences using this easy-to-use service. I enjoy the diversification of REITs, but if establishing a real estate empire is your long-term aim, these guys will help you achieve it—one property at a time.

18. Buy Part of a Farm

Invest in America's farms with AcreTrader, beginning with a $5000 minimum. Since 1990, agricultural investments have enjoyed an 11.5% yearly return (according to the site) (according to the site).

AcreTrader crowdfunds the acquisition of operational farmland and then leases it back to the farmers who run it. Investors gain money in two ways:

appreciation of the property in the case of a future sale\annual cash rent payments from farmers

The corporation targets yearly cash dividends in the 3-5% area.

Curious about more alternative investments? Play around with this fascinating tool to discover what more is out there:

19. Buy a Cash-Flowing Business
Since 50% of all new firms fail within the first 5 years, maybe it makes sense to acquire one that's previously proved profitable.

You may shop on sites like BizBuySell to uncover possibilities near you. Expect to spend 2-3x the yearly profits as a purchase price, but you can generally finance up to 90% of the sale with an SBA loan.

My buddy joined me on the show to discuss the merits of purchasing a company vs. investing in real estate and gives a course on the issue called Unconventional Acquisitions.

20. Buy a Cash-Flowing Website
As I can verify, blogs and websites may make amazing passive revenue without your direct participation. But you also normally can't remain still for long before that revenue begins to vanish.

Things fail, the information requires updating, and Google rankings are continually changing.

Still, if you have online skills, you may appreciate this interview with Stacy Caprio. She acquired enough cash flow in the form of existing websites from the Flippa marketplace to leave her job.

21. Flip Raw Land
To be true, this passive income plan takes a ton of effort initially but if done well, you'll be receiving dividends for years.

The fundamental concept, as outlined by Roberto Chavez on The Side Hustle Show, is to acquire pieces of unoccupied land at a discount, and then to re-sell that property on a monthly payment schedule.

22. Sell Printables

If you don't happen to be sitting on mountains of idle cash, the good news is there are still lots of ways you can begin building a passive income.

I think committing part of your time to just one goal is highly useful. When the assets you construct start paying off, you may steadily taper off exchanging time for money.

One of them is passive income options selling printables via a site like Etsy. Side Hustle Show guest Rachel Jones reported selling up to $10,000 a month worth of these digital files!

(Think meal plans, intake forms, chore schedules, budgeting templates, etc.)

23. Rent Out Your Extra Stuff

Your Car

The typical automobile sits idle for approximately \s(22) hours a day. What if you could transform the time you didn't need your automobile into cash flow?

That's the promise of peer-to-peer car rental platforms like Turo and Getaround. These markets make it simple to advertise your car for hire, choose your fees, and be paid—and they handle all the insurance.

Some friends of mine earned enough to cover the cost of a Tesla! Along the way, they've developed several methods to secure their "fleet" and reduce their time.

Your RV

The "idle time" numbers for RVs are considerably worse than for vehicles. If you've got an RV parked in your side yard, it could make sense to let another family take it for a ride.

Sites like RVShare offer peer-to-peer rentals and provide insurance. The costs vary from $150-300 a night!

Your Boat
With sites like Boatsetter and GetMyBoat, you can rent your boat to your landlocked peers. A simple search of boats nearby gave lots of options with fees ranging from $230 to $950 per day!

How frequently do you go out on the water?

Your Stuff
A variety of markets have cropped up to help you generate money from products you seldom use, and to stop borrowers avoid purchasing equipment they don't need.

One popular outlet is Babyquip, which leases excellent used baby gear to traveling families. Members average over $600 a month in rental revenue.

Meanwhile, FatLlama has gone wider, employing the motto "Airbnb for your stuff."

24. Subcontract a Service Business

Chris Schwab started a residential house cleaning business back when he was still in college. In less than two years, he'd grown it to $60,000 a month—all while never mopping a floor or dusting a shelf himself.

Despite hundreds of rival cleaning businesses, Chris recognized there was still a possibility. He figured it out while studying Yelp evaluations of current cleaning businesses.

"No one complained about the cleaning itself," he claimed. "What people complained about was the customer service. They didn't know when the team was going to come up; they couldn't obtain a price; no one was answering the phone. I knew I could accomplish that, and hire cleaners to perform the real work."

Since then, he's delegated most of the customer support as well. When we caught up, the company required only a few minutes a day for him to handle.

25. Set up a Drop Shipping Store

Drop shipping is a unique type of e-commerce where your supplier ships the products to customers on your behalf. As the vendor, you don't have to acquire any merchandise until you have a buyer. Your profit comes from the difference between the retail price you charge and the wholesale price you've agreed upon with your supplier.

Although there is a lot of initial effort in developing the site and securing supplier partnerships, drop shipping may be quite passive after that.

26. Set Up a Vending Machine

Vending machines are one of the oldest passive income concepts. They're machines that gather money while you're not around!

The problem is managing inventory and keeping the machines filled, particularly if you have many sites. Still, the prospect of returning to a machine and finding it stocked with money is extremely compelling.

For more on how the vending machine company may work, check out my interview with Matt Miller, whose passive income empire began with only $36 and a bag of gumballs.

27. License Your Work

Product licensing is a unique way to make residual money from your ideas—while letting someone else perform the labor.

For example, Wells and his brother shared $300,000 in royalties on a Pictionary-inspired card game they licensed to Mattel.

The pair (a dentist and a preacher) didn't have to develop it, make it, or sell it—but they found someone who could—and they paid the checks.

Other items you may license:

Photography\sMusic\sVoice over work

28. Develop an App or Software

Could you tackle an issue using the software? It's the ideal scalable company in that the same underlying code may be sold to an indefinite number of clients.

A premium software product may be marketed either as a one-off purchase or a recurring monthly subscription.

As a consumer, I've purchased both smartphone applications and desktop software. If you don't have the technical skills to construct something like this yourself, you could always collaborate or employ someone who does—or white-label software that already exists. The key aspect is to conduct your investigation upfront and make sure there's a voracious market need for what you're developing.

Look to tools like AppSumo or ProductHunt to achieve early momentum.

29. Develop an Alexa Skill
There are a few ways side hustlers may generate passive revenue using Amazon's famous Echo gadgets.

The first is like Apple's app store. You can design customized Alexa voice applications, called "skills."

As a talent creator, you can establish your pricing and receive 70% of the money when people purchase it. For example, Nick Schwab has 10,000 paying clients for ambient noise expertise. He produced a free version for individuals to trial, and priced the premium version at $0.99 and $1.99 a month.

Amazon also offers a rewards scheme to encourage developers to expand the ecosystem of skills. The benefits are depending on the popularity and engagement of your talent, and some developers claim to make hundreds of dollars a month.

30. Rent Your Bandwidth

New software called Honeygain has been creating a lot of "buzz" recently. According to the site, users may earn up to $30 a month when they share "your unused net traffic with data scientists."

After you install the program (available for Windows, macOS, and Android), connect it to the Internet, and collect prizes passively. On average, it takes users 48 days to achieve $20.

Get a $5 incentive to start.

Before you get started, however, make sure you're genuinely on an unlimited plan since it seems like this might eat up a lot of data fast!

31. Invest in Small Businesses
To add variety and cash flow to my portfolio, I've taken up a minor holding in Worthy Bonds.

These small company bonds yield 5% interest, and you can purchase them for just

$10 each. The bonds are intended to support inventory or asset-backed loans to small U.S. enterprises.

Since the loans employ goods as security, they're deemed safer than conventional personal or corporate loans. You may also automatically re-invest your interest and make penalty-free withdrawals at any time.

Unfortunately, at press time Worthy is sold out of fresh bonds but you may sign up to receive alerts when they obtain clearance to offer more.

The 4 Types of Passive Income

The appeal of passive income is alluring. I mean, if the prospect of generating money in your sleep doesn't make you thrilled, I'd check your pulse.

On top of that, passive income is vital.

I'll let Warren Buffett explain:

"If you don't find a way to make money while you sleep, you will work until you die."

I think we can all get on board with that.

So how can you get some of that sweet, sweet passive income—or "mailbox money"—for yourself?

Here's what you need to know.

In general, passive income is the money you earn from assets you control. (Assets are simply things that other people value; cash, real estate, tangible items, attention, etc.)

The negative is assets generally require either time to construct or money to acquire.

Here are the 4 forms of passive income you may start working toward today:

1. Buy cash-flowing assets

This is the "make money with money" option. Under this category, you'll find options like dividend investing, business lending, real estate, and stuff like that.

It's great—if you already have money to invest!

2. Build assets

Building something of value—say, a digital product or website that earns advertising revenue—is a viable path to passive income. These things take some time to create and market, but can run relatively passively often for years if set up correctly.

3. Share or sell assets

There are methods to create relatively-passive income by renting or selling things you own.

This may be spare space around your home, objects you have accumulating dust or even the data created by your phone.

4. "Reverse" passive income

"Reverse" passive income comes from cutting your ongoing monthly expenses. A penny saved is a penny earned, right?

Well, because of taxes on earned income, it's better than that! And there's no extreme couponing required.

Why Passive Income Ideas Matter

I'm not an investment guru or financial wizard, but the vast majority of my income is "passive"—or at least time-leveraged.

By time-leveraged, I mean I don't punch a clock or trade my time for money in any direct way.

I began my career the way most people do—with a job. But over time, I've purposefully created more passive income sources, while raising the total size of the revenue pie as well.

The little sliver of "active income" on the chart comes from one-on-one consultancy calls.

Unfortunately, here's how the chart appears for most people:

They have a substantial piece of active income—from their job—and (if they're fortunate) a modest slice of investment income.

Let's work toward shifting the balance to the green!

It's crucial to note I've built things up progressively over time, beginning when I was still working a 9-5 job. I don't want to convey the idea that I'm raking in millions